A Handbook for Aliens to Remain Legal in the United States

by

Olusegun Asekun

authorHOUSE™

1663 Liberty Drive, Suite 200
Bloomington, Indiana 47403
(800) 839-8640
www.AuthorHouse.com

First published by AuthorHouse 04/13/05

ISBN: 1-4208-4573-X (sc)

Printed in the United States of America
Bloomington, Indiana

This book is printed on acid-free paper.

The Law Offices of Olu Asekun
607 East Abram Street, Suite 9
Arlington Texas, 76010, USA
Tel.: 817-274-1144
817-819-3459
Fax: 817-274-1101
www.olufairdeal.org
E-mail: info@olufairdeal.org

DEDICATION

This book is dedicated to God, and to thousands of aliens who are suffering in silence due to lack of knowledge of what to do. My prayer is that my work will help bring them out of their sufferings.

Table of Contents

LEGAL DISCLAIMER

IMMIGRATION LAW IS CONSTANTLY CHANGING. THEREFORE THE INFORMATIONS PROVIDED IN THIS BOOK ARE INTENDED FOR INFORMATIONAL PURPOSES ONLY. IT IS PROVIDED "AS IS" WITHOUT ANY WARRANTY, EXPRESSED OR IMPLIED. THESE INFORMATIONS ARE NOT SUBSTITUTED FOR LEGAL ADVICE.

INTRODUCTION

Many individuals around the world will do anything to come to America. Some sell properties, some borrow money, some even change their identities just to procure a visa to "God's own country. In some cases some people "arrange" marriages; some "arrange" employment.

There are also other cases of desperate situation where human beings are loaded as goods in commercial non-ventilated trucks and, or trailers. Some are smuggled into the United States to escape persecution in their own Country. People therefore trooped into the United States in search of freedom, greener pastures, and or opportunity.

In some countries bad leadership, civil war, and, or corruption have eroded the hope of the common man. America is widely regarded as a land of freedom and opportunity, hence the need to exploit the opportunity. Immigration statistics shows that over

125 million I-94 documented non-immigrants were admitted between 1999 and 2002. Of this figure, over 86% entered as visitors.

Some immigrants become illegal and undocumented *ab initio* because they entered the United States "uninspected". Some however came into the United States legally and documented but later become illegal either out of carelessness or lack of knowledge of what to do.

More often than none, the alien's host determines the future of the alien. In other words, what the alien will do or omit to do depends on the knowledge of the host. This is because *"nemo dat quad non habet"* (you cannot give what you don't have).

In some cases, the host would innocently discourage the alien from taking the right step thereby compounding the alien's problems. In other cases, fear factor causes the problem. In all this cases, ignorance is a major contributory factor.

Everywhere legal system is operative all over the world, it is generally accepted that "ignorance of the Law is no excuse". Even for those that believe in the Bible, the Bible also says "my people perish for lack of knowledge". It is therefore important that you acquire knowledge of your new environment.

In my short but fruitful immigration law practice in the United States, I have come across people who are facing immigration problem today just because of lack of knowledge of what to do.

Some of these people are so ignorant to the extent that they fall victim to people of dubious characters. Recently, thousand of people went to Florida in search of employment authorization document. It was too late by the time some of them, if not all, realized that they should not have done that.

In the same vein, I have come across people who think it cost fortune to consult an attorney for professional advice. It is with this in mind that it became a burden in my mind to provide an accessible handbook on how to maintain legal status

CHAPTER ONE
DETERMINE YOUR STATUS

DID YOU ENTER THE UNITED STATES INSPECTED?

What this simply means is – did you obtain a visa from any American Embassy abroad to enter the United States, or are you from a visa waiver country? If yes, were you issued I-94 at the port of entry? I-94 is the arrival departure record card you complete at port of entry.

The immigration official will stamp your authorized stay on this card. The number of days, weeks, months, or years depends on the purpose of your coming to the United States, and it is entirely at the discretion of the immigration officer at the port of entry.

Usually alien from visa waiver countries are allowed to stay for a period not exceeding three months (90 days). Alien with B1/B2 visa (Visitors for business or pleasure) are allowed to stay in the United States for a period ranging from one week to six months depending on the purpose of visit.

Where there is a good reason for doing so, the period of authorized stay may be renewed for a maximum period of six months at a time. In addition, in very rare cases, some alien with a visitor's visa may be granted an extension of stay for a second time.

Majority of immigrants enter the United States as a visitor and subsequently change their status. An alien becomes out of status once the authorized stay expires except he/she has taken step to either extend it or change status.

If you entered the United States without this Form I-94 card, it simply means you entered the United States uninspected.

ARE YOU STILL IN STATUS?

Having determined that you came into the United States inspected, the next step is to determine if you are still in status. To remain in status, you must <u>not</u> remain in the United States for a day longer than the number of days, weeks, or months stamped on your I-94 <u>except</u> you have taken step either to extend your authorized stay or in the process of changing your status.

Being in the process of changing your status means that you have an application pending with Citizenship and Immigration Services (C.I.S.) formerly known as Immigration and Naturalization Services (I.N.S.) or Bureau of Citizenship and Immigration Services (B.C.I.S.). Whether or not the application has been approved is immaterial at this stage. The point to note is that for as long as your application has not been denied, you are still in status.

Once again, in determining whether or not you are in status, for the purpose of change of status, the merit of your application is immaterial at this stage. However, it must be pointed out that your being in status is subject to your change of status application being approved before your application for extension is either approved or denied.

Where your application for extension of stay is approved after your change of status application is filed, but yet to be determined, you would still be in status for the purpose of your change of status application. On the other hand, where the application for extension of stay is denied after your change of status application is filed, but yet to be determined, then your change of status application may be denied on the ground that you are out of status.

In addition, where the alien can provide satisfactory evidence of a genuine reason for failure to file either an application for extension or change of status within the authorized period of stay, such application, if filed within a reasonable time after the expiration of I-94 may still be accepted as validly filed. However, the decision here is discretionary. It is only if the immigration officer is satisfied with your reason for not filing your application on time.

A lot of people have become illegal alien out of the erroneous belief that they are out of status once the I-94 (Arrival/Departure record) expires even when they have an application for extension or change of status pending. It is advisable that you seek legal advice where you are in doubt.

DOES UNEXPIRED VISA KEEP YOU IN STATUS?

No. There is a difference between a visa and the Form I-94. A visa is usually obtained outside the United States. Precisely at the American embassy at the alien's country. It is usually useful outside the United States. It is the license that authorizes the Airline to carry the alien. It is not more than that.

A visa does not even guarantee the alien's admission into the United States. Admission is still subject to the discretion of the immigration officers at the port of entry. A visa is not useful for the purpose of maintaining status in the United States.

On the other hand, the immigration officer at the port of entry issues a Form I-94 card solely for the purpose of informing the alien of the specific number of weeks and months he is authorized to stay in the United States. A form I-94 card is therefore not useful outside the United States.

The significance of this distinction is to let the alien be aware that the fact that your visa has not expired does not keep you in status in the United States, especially if your Form I-94 card has expired.

Remember, ignorance of the Law is no excuse. However, a further explanation about being in status is necessary before I go further. The following scenario will explain it better.

SCENE A

An alien entered the United States on January 3rd, 2000 through JFK International Airport in New York. At the port of entry (JFK), she was issued Form I-94 authorizing her to stay in the United States till July 2nd, 2000 (Six months). On July 1st, she filed an application to extend her authorized stay.

Question 1: Is the alien still in status?

Answer: Yes. But it is <u>not</u> advisable that the alien should wait till the last minute. Alien should file application for extension as soon as she become aware that she may not depart the United States within the authorized period.

Question 2: While the application for extension of stay is pending, can the alien file application for change of status?

Answer : Yes. However, the success is subject to the application being determined before the application for extension of status. It is therefore advisable that the alien or petitioner takes advantage of premium processing program, where available. (Read Scene B for further clarification)

Question 3: Assume that after filing the application for extension of authorized stay, C.I.S. (Immigration) request additional evidence in support of the application, can the alien file an application for change of status before responding to the request for evidence?

Answer : Yes. Application for change of status can be filed for as long as the application for extension of authorized stay has not been denied. However, it must be pointed out that the success of her application is subject to her new application being determined before her application to extend her visitor status is denied. It is therefore advisable that the alien takes advantage of premium processing program where applicable. In addition, it is advisable that alien seek expert advise from experienced immigration attorney if in doubt.

Question 4: What if the application for change of status had been filed before the expiration of the original I-94?

Answer: The issue of being out of status does not arise in the first place if you file application for change of status while your I-94 is still current

SCENE B

After filing application for extension, the alien received a request for additional evidence but before responding to the request, a U.S. based Company decided to file an H-1B status for the alien.

Question 5: Is the alien still in status for the purpose of the H-1B?

Answer : Yes. However, the success of the H-1B depends on whether or not the H-1B application is determined before the application for extension is either granted or denied. Where the application for extension is approved, it does not have any negative impact on the H-1B application.

However, where the application for extension is denied, it would not have any negative impact on the H-1B application only if the application for extension has not been denied at the time the H-1B is determined.

Consequently, it is advisable that the petitioner takes advantage of the premium-processing program where applicable. Note that where the application to be filed does not come under the premium-processing program, for instance, H-4 application by the dependant of an H-1B status, the application may not be approved, especially if the application for extension is denied at any stage before the H4 petition is approved. It is immaterial that the application for H-4 was filed before the application for extension is denied.

Question 6: Assume that the alien filed an application for extension on July 1st for himself

and his wife. By September 15, while the application for extension is yet to be denied, an H-1B status was filed for the alien using premium processing program, and H-4 for the wife, what are the chances of approval as it affects being in status?

Answer : As for the H1B, considering the use of premium processing program, if the application is determined before the application for extension is determined, the H-1B may be approved. In addition, if the H-4 application is filed concurrently with the H-1B application, the chance is that it would also enjoy the benefits of premium processing.

Similarly, if the application for extension is approved, it means that the applicant is still in status at the time of filing the application, and therefore, the both applications may still be approved.

Question 7: Assume that the alien filed an application for extension of status on July 1st 2003 requesting for extension of stay for a period of six months. By March 2004, the application is yet to be approved or denied, the alien then filed an application for change of status, what is the probability of success?

Answer: The application for change of status is likely to be denied on the ground that the alien is out of status. This is because the period of extension requested by the alien has passed. This means that even where the application for extension is approved, the period of authorized extension (December, 2003) would have expired.

Question 8: Assume that the application for extension of authorized stay is denied; can the alien file an application for change of status?

Answer: No (However, you can contact an Attorney to determine other benefits)

It must be pointed out that all applications does not qualify to keep the alien in status even where they are filed on time. Example of such applications are I-130 filed by a Permanent Resident or what is also known as Green Card holder for alien spouse or minor children.

In other words, the fact that the application was filed while an alien was still in status is immaterial. I-130 filed by a Green Card holder does not keep the alien in status. (Contact an Attorney for further details on this).

In addition, a Religious worker who has been on R-1 and who filed Form I-360 (Special Immigrant Religious worker would not be maintaining lawful legal status simply by filing the Form I-360 where the R-1 has expired. Consequently, such alien should file application to extend the R-1 while waiting for the Form I-360 application to be determined. It must be pointed out that an alien can stay on R-1 for a maximum period of five years.

CHAPTER TWO
DETERMINE IF YOU
CAN CHANGE STATUS

CAN ALL ALIEN IN STATUS CHANGE THEIR STATUS?

No. Apart from maintaining a legal status, certain factors will still disqualify an alien in legal status from changing status in the United States. The most important of these factors is criminal activity. An alien who fails to obey the laws of the United States by engaging in criminal activities for which a sentence of more than one-year imprisonment may be imposed is disqualified not only from changing status but also from remaining legally in the Country.

Apart from criminal activities, an alien who failed to maintain the previously accorded status or where such status expired before the application or petition was filed, except that failure to file before the period of previously authorized status expired may be excused in the discretion of Immigration Service, where it is demonstrated at the time of filing that:

1   The delay was due to extraordinary circumstances beyond the control of the applicant or petitioner, and the Service finds the delay commensurate with the circumstances.

2   The alien has not otherwise violated his or her nonimmigrant status.

3   The alien remains a bona fide nonimmigrant.

4   The alien is not the subject of deportation proceedings.

In addition, an alien in a nonimmigrant status may not engage in any employment in the United States unless he has been accorded a nonimmigrant classification, which authorizes employment, or he has been granted permission to engage in employment by Immigration.

A nonimmigrant that is permitted to engage in employment may engage only in such employment as has been authorized. Any unauthorized employment by a nonimmigrant constitutes a failure to maintain status under Immigration law.

In general, you may apply to change your nonimmigrant status if you were lawfully admitted into the United States with a nonimmigrant visa and your nonimmigrant status remains valid, and you have not committed any crimes that would make you ineligible.

ARE ALL CATEGORIES OF VISA ELIGIBLE FOR CHANGE OF STATUS?

No. Some visa categories are not eligible for change of status. People admitted to the United States in any of these categories may **NOT** change their nonimmigrant status in the United States:

- Visa Waiver Pilot Program (or the Guam Visa Waiver Program).

- Crewman

- Alien in transit or in transit without a visa.

- Fiancée or spouse of a U.S. citizen or dependent of a fiancée or spouse. This is because a fiancée or spouse of a U.S. citizen is seen as a potential immigrant, and not a non-immigrant. They should therefore apply to register permanent residence instead of changing non-immigrant status.

- Informant and accompanying family on terrorism or organized crime.

- International exchange visitor (J visa category) may not change her nonimmigrant status if she was admitted to the United States to receive graduate medical training, unless she receive a special waiver.

In addition, some exchange visitors must meet a foreign residence requirement before they are allowed to change status. This means that some international exchange visitors must leave the United States and go back to their home country for a minimum of two years before applying to come to the United States as a temporary worker or an immigrant.

An exchange visitor required to meet the foreign residence requirement, must receive a waiver if she wish to change nonimmigrant status without returning home. If you do not receive a waiver, then you may only apply to change to the A (Diplomatic and other government officials, and their families and employees) or G (Representatives to international organizations and their families and employees) nonimmigrant categories.

If you are a vocational student (M visa category), you may not apply to become an academic student (F visa category). You also may not apply to change from the vocational student visa category to a temporary worker visa category (H) if it was the training you received as a vocational student in the United States that made you qualified for the temporary worker position. However, if you are already qualified before you entered the United States, you can change your status to H category.

If you are in the United States as the spouse or child of someone in any of the following nonimmigrant visa categories, and you wish to attend school in the United States, you do not need to change your status before you can go to school (as long as your parent or spouse maintains their original nonimmigrant status).

- **A** - Diplomatic and other government officials, and their families and employees.

- **E** - International Trade and Investors.

- **G** - Representatives to international organizations and their families and employees.

- **H & R** - Temporary Workers.

- **I** - Representatives of foreign media and their families.

- **J** - Exchange Visitors and their families.

- **L** – Intra-company Transferees

If you are in the United States as the spouse or child of someone in the F (Academic Student) or M (Vocational Student) visa category, you do not need to apply to change your status if you wish to attend elementary, middle, or high school in the United States. If you wish to attend post-secondary school full-time, you must change your status.

CHAPTER THREE
WHAT ARE THE
OPTIONS AVAILABLE?

NON-IMMIGRANT OR
TEMPORARY CATEGORY

Now that you have determined that you entered the United States inspected and that you are still in status, you need to know what options are available. There are two categories of options under the Immigration laws. They are non immigrant and Immigrant. The basic difference in the two is that non-immigrant is temporary while immigrant is permanent.

An alien in a non immigrant status is expected to go back to his last country of residence abroad at the end of the period of authorized stay in the United States except the alien has changed her status from non immigrant to immigrant, or is in the process of doing so.

In other words, if the alien has filed an application to register permanent residence or adjust status (Form I-485) before the expiration of the period of authorized stay, she may not leave the U.S. at the end of the period of authorized stay.

The following are some of the non-immigrant options available.

NON-IMMIGRANT STATUS

E VISA

An alien entitled to enter the United States under and in pursuance of the provisions of a treaty of commerce and navigation between the United States and the foreign state, of which he is a national, and the spouse and children of any such alien if accompanying or following to join him solely to carry on substantial trade, including trade in services or trade in technology, principally between the United States and the foreign state of which he is a national, or solely to develop and direct the operations of an enterprise in which he has invested, or of an enterprise in which he is actively in the process of investing, a substantial amount of capital.

F-1 VISA

F-1 Visa is a student visa issued to foreign nationals wishing to pursue a full time academic course of study at an accredited institution in the U.S. It is usually valid for the duration of study (D/S). However, it must be pointed out that non-attendance of school invalidates the status, even if it is for one semester

H-1B VISA

H-1B Visa is a work visa generally used by Professionals to be employed in a specialty occupation. The beneficiary must have a minimum of a bachelor's degree or its equivalent and the job must also require a bachelor's degree or its equivalent. It is usually granted for initial 3 years and renewable for another 3 years (Maximum of 6 years). The spouse and the minor children of the holder may be entitled to H-4 dependent visas.

Alien needs a sponsor company to file H-1B. Alien cannot file for himself. Currently, there is a 65,000 yearly cap on this type of visa. What this means is that only 65,000 aliens are allowed into this category per year. The alien is advised to seek legal advice if you are considering this type of visa

H-1C VISA

Nurses coming to work for up to three years in the United States in an area of health determined to have professional shortage

H2B VISA

An alien who has a residence in a foreign country which he has no intention of abandoning, and who is coming temporarily to the United States to perform agricultural labor or services. Temporary services or labor under the H-2B classification refers to any job in which the petitioner's need for the duties to be performed by the employee(s) is temporary, whether or not the underlying job can be described as permanent or temporary. It is usually for a period of ten months

H-3 VISA

H-3 Visa is for foreign nationals coming temporarily to receive training from a U.S. employer in any field other than graduate education. It is valid for 2years under this category and is not subject to renewal. It may also be used to participate in a special education training program in the education of children with physical, mental and, or emotional disabilities. It is valid for 18months under this category and is not subject to renewal

I VISA

Upon a basis of reciprocity, an alien who is a bona fide representative of foreign press, radio, film, or other foreign information media, who seeks to enter the United States solely to engage in such vocation, and the spouse and children of such a representative if accompanying or following to join him.

J VISA

An alien having a residence in a foreign country which he has no intention of abandoning who is a bona fide student, scholar, trainee, teacher, professor, research assistant, specialist, or leader in a field of specialized knowledge or skill, or other person of similar description, who is coming temporarily to the United States as a participant in a program designated by the Director of the United States Information Agency, for the purpose of teaching, instructing or lecturing, studying, observing, conducting research, consulting, demonstrating special skills, or receiving training and who, if he is coming to the United States to participate in a program under which he will receive graduate medical education or training and the alien spouse and minor children of any such alien if accompanying him or following to join him

K VISA

K Visa enables the spouse or fiancée of an American citizen to come, live, and work in the U.S. temporarily until the I-130 Petition for alien relative is approved, or in the case of fiancée until the alien is married to the American citizen, usually within 90 days. In the case of fiancée visa, the American citizen and the fiancée must have met physically within the last two years immediately preceding the filing of the petition

L-1A VISA

L-1A Visa is a visa for managers or executives to work at a U.S. Company related to the foreign Company where they have worked as a manager or executive for a minimum of 1 year within the 3 years preceding the application. It is for initial 3 years and renewable for up to 7 years in increment of 2 years. Where the Company's office in the U.S. is new, it is granted for initial 1 year but renewable for up to a total of 7years

M-1 VISA

M-1 Visa is also a student visa. However, this is available to foreign nationals wishing to pursue non-academic or vocational studies in the U.S. It is also valid for duration of study (D/S)

O VISA

An alien who has extraordinary ability in the sciences, arts, education, business, or athletics which has been demonstrated by sustained national or international acclaim or, with regard to motion picture and television productions a demonstrated record of extraordinary achievement.

The achievements must have been recognized in the field through extensive documentation, and seeks to enter the United States to continue work in the area of extraordinary ability, or performs as an artist or entertainer, individually or as part of a group, or is an integral part of the performance of such a group.

He must seek to enter the United States temporarily and solely for the purpose of performing as such an artist or entertainer or with such a group under a reciprocal exchange program which is between an organization or organizations in the United States and an organization or organizations in one or more foreign states and which provides for the temporary exchange of artists and entertainers, performs as an artist or entertainer, individually or as part of a group, or is an integral part of the performance of such a group. He must seek to enter the United States temporarily and solely to perform, teach, or coach as such an artist or entertainer or with such a group under a commercial or noncommercial program that is culturally unique.

Q VISA

An alien having a residence in a foreign country which he has no intention of abandoning who is coming temporarily (for a period not to exceed 15 months) to the United States as a participant in an international cultural exchange program approved by the Attorney General for the purpose of providing practical training, employment, and the sharing of the history, culture, and traditions of the country of the alien's nationality and who will be employed under the same wages and working conditions as domestic workers.

R-1

R-1 Visa is a work visa that allows Religious workers to work temporarily for a religious organization recognized as such in the U.S. It is granted for an initial 3 years and renewable for additional 2 years. To qualify, the alien must have been a member of the sponsoring Religious organization for a minimum period of 2 years.

Alternatively, if the U.S. Religious organization and the foreign Religious denomination belong to the same denominations, the 2-year requirement may be satisfied with evidence that the alien has been with the foreign Religious denomination for a minimum period of 2 years.

TN

TN Visa is a work visa granted to citizens of Canada or Mexico to work in a professional occupation in the U.S. The profession must be on the list of North American Free Trade Agreement (NAFTA). The visa is valid for one year at a time. Currently, there is no limit to the number of times it can be renewed.

V- VISA

V-Visa allows spouse or unmarried child less than 21 years of age of a lawful permanent resident to live and work in the U.S. in a non-immigrant category. Applicant must have filed form I-130 on or before December 21, 2000. Visa is valid until the I-485 is approved.

TEMPORARY PROTECTED STATUS

Temporary Protected Status (TPS) is a temporary immigration status granted to eligible nationals of designated countries (or parts thereof). In 1990, Congress established a procedure by which the Attorney General may provide TPS to aliens in the United States who are temporarily unable to return to their homeland because of ongoing-armed conflict, environmental disasters, or other extraordinary and temporary conditions.

During the period for which the Attorney General has designated a country under the TPS program, TPS beneficiaries are not required to leave the United States and may obtain work authorization. However, TPS does not lead to permanent resident status.

When the Attorney General terminates a country's TPS designation, beneficiaries return to the same immigration status they maintained before TPS (unless that status had since expired or been terminated) or to any other status they may have acquired while registered for TPS.

Accordingly, if an alien had unlawful status prior to receiving TPS and did not obtain any status during the TPS period, she/he will revert to that unlawful status upon the termination of that TPS designation.

Eligibility for TPS

An alien who is a national of a country (or alien having no nationality who last habitually resided in that country) designated by the Attorney General is eligible to apply for benefits under the TPS program if he or she establishes continuous physical presence and continuous residence in the United States for a specified period of time, is not subject to several criminal and security-related bars, and timely registers for TPS benefits.

If the Attorney General extends a TPS designation beyond the initial designation period, the beneficiary must timely re-register to maintain his or her benefits under the TPS program.

CHAPTER FOUR
IMMIGRANT CATEGORY

You may be eligible to apply for adjustment to permanent resident status if you are already in the United States and if one or more of the following categories apply to you.

FAMILY BASED PETITION

- You are the spouse, parent, unmarried child under age 21, the unmarried son or daughter over age 21, the married son or daughter, or the brother or sister of a United States citizen and have a visa petition approved in your behalf.

- You are the spouse or unmarried son or daughter of any age of a lawful permanent resident and you have a family-based visa petition approved in your behalf.

OTHERWISE ELIGIBLE
IMMEDIATE RELATIVES

Otherwise eligible immediate relative refers to the spouse of an American citizen who entered the United States legally but over stayed the period of authorized admission contained in her I-94 (Arrival/ Departure Record). For the purpose of this provision, it is immaterial whether the alien became the spouse of a U.S. Citizen before or after the expiration of her I-94.

What is important is that the alien entered the United States inspected, and is legally and genuinely married to the American citizen, in which case the alien may adjust to Legal Permanent Resident (green card holder) in the United States even if the alien may have done any of the following:

- Worked without permission

- Remained in the U.S. past the period of lawful admission (e.g. past the expiration date on your I-94) and filed for adjustment of status while in an unlawful status because of that.

- Failed otherwise to maintain lawful status and with the proper immigration documentation.

- Have been admitted as a visitor without a visa under sections 212(l) or 217 of the Act (which are the 15-day admission under the Guam visa waiver program and the 90-day admission under the Visa Waiver Program, respectively).

NOTE: IF A PERSON CAME INTO THE U.S. ILLEGALLY, (WITHOUT INSPECTION, SEE CHAPTER ONE) THAT PERSON IS BARRED FROM ADJUSTING THEIR STATUS EVEN IF THE PERSON MARRIES A U.S. CITIZEN.

IN OTHER WORDS, IF YOU ENTERED THE U.S ILLEGALLY, THERE IS NO IMMIGRATION BENEFIT AVAILABLE TO YOU EVEN IF YOU WIN THE VISA LOTTERY.

In addition, the following categories of people CANNOT adjust their status, except you are the immediate relative of a U.S. citizen (parent, spouse, or unmarried child under 21 years old) or you fall into the category of foreign medical graduates in shortage areas or international organization employees and family members.

- You entered the U.S. while you were in transit to another country without obtaining a U.S. visa.

- You entered the U.S. while you were a nonimmigrant crewman.

- You were not admitted or paroled into the United States after being inspected by a U.S.

Immigration inspector.

- You are employed in the United States without USCIS authorization or you are no longer legally in the country (except through no fault of your own or for some technical reason).

- You are a J-1 or J-2 exchange visitor who must comply with the two-year foreign residence requirement, except you have met or been granted a waiver for this requirement.

- You have an A (diplomatic status), E (treaty trader or investor), or G (representative to international organization) nonimmigrant status, or have an occupation that would allow you have this status. This rule will not apply to you if you complete USCIS Form I-508 (I-508F for French nationals) to waive diplomatic rights, privileges and immunities. If you are an A or G nonimmigrant, you must also submit USCIS Form I-566.

- You were admitted to Guam as a visitor under the Guam Visa Waiver Program. (This does not apply to immediate relatives.)

- You were admitted into the United States as a visitor under the Visa Waiver

Program. (This rule does not apply to you if you are the immediate relative of a U.S. citizen (parent, spouse, or unmarried child under 21).)

- You are already a conditional permanent resident.

- You were admitted as a K-1 fiancé but did not marry the U.S. citizen who filed the petition for you. Or, you were admitted as the K-2 child of a fiancé and your parent did not marry the U.S. citizen who filed the petition for you.

Under the family category, it is now possible in some areas to get a permanent resident status (green card) within 90 days. This program is called pilot program. As at the time of sending this work to the publishers, the pilot program is available in Dallas office. It is known as Dallas Office Rapid Adjustment Program (D.O.R.A.)

DOCUMENTATIONS

Where the beneficiary is present in the United States, and is applying under the family category (spouse), she will need the following documentations:

FEES (Fees are subject to change at the discretion of C.I.S.)

1. $315 Money order for I-485

2. $185 Money order for I-130
3. $70 Money order for Fingerprinting

FORMS

4. Completed I-485 App. to Register Permanent Residence or Adjust Status
5. Completed Form I-130 Petition for Alien Relative
6. Completed form I-864 Affidavit of support
7. Medical Examination of the alien
8. Completed Form G-325 Biographic information: Husband
9. Completed Form G-325 Biographic information: Wife

NECESSARY DOCUMENTS

A. COMPULSORY

a. Copies of Birth Certificate: Both parties
10. Copy of Naturalization Certificate, if applicable
11. Copy of Visa page of passport
12. Copy of I-94
13. Copy of Data page of Travel Passport:
14. 2 Passport photographs each
15. Copy of Marriage License/Certificate
16. Copy of proof of Termination of earlier Marriage, if any
17. Copies of 3 years Tax documents

B. REQUIRED (YOU MAY NOT HAVE ALL BUT YOU MUST HAVE SOME)

18. Proof of joint Bank Account
19. Proof of Joint Credit Card
20. Proof of Joint Loans
21. Proof of Joint Lease/Mortgage
22. Proof of Joint Utility Bills-water, gas, light, phone, cable, etc
23. Life insurance with spouse as beneficiary
24. Joint auto insurance
25. Birth Certificate of children
26. Wedding album

Where the beneficiary is outside the United States, she will need to submit the following documentations before immigrant visa can be issued to her:

1. Passport photographs
2. Birth certificates
3. Police certificates
4. Fingerprint
5. Affidavit of Support
6. Medical Examinations. Before the issuance of an immigrant visa, every applicant, regardless of age, must undergo a medical examination. A doctor designated by the consular officer will conduct the examination. Examination costs must be borne by the applicant, in addition to the visa fees.

NOTE

Whenever there are more qualified applicants for a category than there are available numbers, the category will be considered oversubscribed, and immigrant visas will be issued in the chronological order in which the petitions were filed until the numerical limit for the category is reached.

The filing date of a petition becomes the applicant's priority date. Immigrant visas cannot be issued until an applicant's priority date is reached. In certain heavily oversubscribed categories, there may be a waiting period of several years before a priority date is reached.

EMPLOYMENT BASED

Employment based permanent resident simply means that a foreign national has been authorized to live and work permanently in the United States. If you want to become an immigrant based on the fact that you have a permanent employment opportunity in the United States, or if you are an employer that wants to sponsor someone for lawful permanent residency based on permanent employment in the United States, you must qualify through one of the following.

ELIGIBILITY

There are five categories for granting permanent residence to foreign nationals based on employment skills.

EB –1 PRIORITY WORKERS

- Foreign nationals of extraordinary ability in the sciences, arts, education, business or athletics

- Foreign national that are outstanding professors or researchers

- Foreign nationals that are managers and executives subject to international transfer to the United States

EB-2 PROFESSIONALS WITH ADVANCED DEGREE OR PERSONS WITH EXCEPTIONAL ABILITY

- Foreign nationals of exceptional ability in the sciences, arts or business

- Foreign nationals that are advanced degree professionals

- Qualified alien physicians who will practice medicine in an area of the U.S., which is underserved.

EB-3 SKILLED OR PROFESSIONAL WORKERS

- Foreign national professionals with bachelor's degrees (not qualifying for a higher preference category)

- Foreign national skilled workers (minimum two years training and experience)

- Foreign national unskilled workers

EB-4 SPECIAL IMMIGRANTS

- Foreign national religious workers (See Chapter Six)

- Employees and former employees of the U.S. Government abroad

EMPLOYMENT BASED
IMMIGRATION PROCEDURE

1. Determine eligibility. In most cases, people who have employment based non-immigrant status eventually graduate to employment based immigrant status.

2. Apply to the U.S. Department of labor. This requires that the U.S. employer complete a labor certification request (Form ETA 750) for the applicant, and submit it to the Department of Labor's Employment and Training Administration. Labor must either grant or deny the certification request.

   Note: Qualified alien physicians who will practice medicine in an area of the United States, which has been certified as underserved by the U.S. Department of Health and Human Services, are relieved from this requirement.

3.   After the approval of the labor certification request, the employer will file Form I-140, Immigrant petition for alien worker.

4.   The State Department must give the applicant an immigrant visa number, even if the applicant is already in the United States. When the applicant receives an immigrant visa number, it means that an immigrant visa has been assigned to the applicant. This simply means that the Form I-140 has been approved.

5.   The applicant may then apply to adjust to permanent resident status by filing Form I-485.

CHAPTER FIVE
OTHER IMMIGRATION
CHANNELS

ASYLUM

Before I define what Asylum is, I wish to warn that **ASYLUM IS ONE OF THE MOST DANGEROUS IMMIGRATION APPLICATIONS**. When an application for Asylum is denied, deportation proceedings is usually commenced against the alien. The information supplied in support of the Asylum application is used against the applicant to deport her, even if the application is withdrawn. It is therefore advisable that applicant should be sure of her facts before applying for Asylum. The front page of Application for Asylum boldly states as follows:

"WARNING: Applicants who are in the United States illegally are subject to removal if their asylum or withholding claims are not granted

by an Asylum Officer or an Immigration Judge. Any information provided in completing this application may be used as a basis for the institution of, or as evidence in, removal proceedings, even if the application is later withdrawn. Applicants determined to have knowingly made a frivolous application for asylum will be permanently ineligible for any benefits under the Immigration and Nationality Act (Act). See Section 208(d)(6) of the Act and 8 CFR 208.20"

Asylum is a form of protection that allows individuals who are in the United States to remain here, provided that they meet the definition of refugee and are not barred from either applying for or being granted asylum, and eventually to adjust their status to lawful permanent resident.

The Immigration Act defines "refugee" as:

(A) any person who is outside any country of such person's nationality or, in the case of a person having no nationality, is outside any country in which such person last habitually resided, and who is unable or unwilling to return to, and is unable or unwilling to avail himself or herself of the protection of, that country because of persecution or a well-founded fear of persecution on account of race, religion, nationality, membership in a particular social group, or political opinion, or

(B) in such circumstances as the President after appropriate consultation, may specify, any person who is within the country of such person's nationality or, in the case of a person having no nationality, within the country in which such person is habitually residing, and who is persecuted or who has a well-founded fear of persecution on account of race, religion, nationality, membership in a particular social group, or political opinion.

The term "refugee" does not include any person who ordered, incited, assisted, or otherwise participated in the persecution of any person on account of race, religion, nationality, membership in a particular social group, or political opinion.

For purposes of determinations under this Act, a person who has been forced to abort a pregnancy or to undergo involuntary sterilization, or who has been persecuted for failure or refusal to undergo such a procedure or for other resistance to a coercive population control program, shall be deemed to have been persecuted on account of political opinion, and a person who has a well founded fear that he or she will be forced to undergo such a procedure or subject to persecution for such failure, refusal, or resistance shall be deemed to have a well founded fear of persecution on account of political opinion.

IMMIGRANT INVESTOR

10,000 immigrant visas per year are available to qualified individuals seeking permanent resident status on the basis of their engagement in a new commercial enterprise. Out of the 10,000-investor visas (i.e., EB-5 visas) available annually, 5,000 are set-aside for those who apply under a pilot program involving a CIS-designated "Regional Center."

A "Regional Center:" is an entity, organization or agency that has been approved as such by the Service and focuses on a specific geographic area within the United States; and, seeks to promote economic growth through increased export sales, improved regional productivity, creation of new jobs, and increased domestic capital investment.

"Alien investors" must demonstrate that a qualified investment is being made in a new commercial enterprise located within an approved Regional Center; and show, using reasonable methodologies, that 10 or more jobs are actually created either directly or indirectly by the new commercial enterprise through revenues generated from increased exports, improved regional productivity, job creation, or increased domestic capital investment resulting from the pilot program.

QUALIFICATION REQUIREMENTS

An investor and his family members (spouse and unmarried children) may be granted Permanent resident status if they fall into one or more of these categories.

1   Those who have invested or are actively in the process of investing at least $1,000,000, (One Million Dollars) or

2 At least $500,000 where the investment is being made in a "targeted employment area," which is an area that has experienced unemployment of at least 150 per cent of the national average rate.

In addition, the investor must further demonstrate that this investment:

a. Will benefit the United States economy and create the requisite number of full-time jobs for qualified persons within the United States.

b. Create full-time employment for not fewer than 10 qualified individuals

c. Maintain the number of existing employees at no less than the pre-investment level for a period of at least two years, where the capital investment is being made in a "troubled business," which is a business that has been in existence for at least two years and that has lost 20 percent of its net worth over the past 12 to 24 months.

Investors may establish a new commercial enterprise by creating an original business or purchase an existing business and simultaneously or subsequently restructuring or reorganizing the business such that a new commercial enterprise results or by expanding an existing business by 140 percent of the pre-investment number of jobs or net worth, or retaining all existing jobs in a troubled business that has lost 20 percent of its net worth over the past 12 to 24 months.

DIVERSITY VISA LOTTERY

Each year, the Diversity Lottery (DV) Program makes 55,000 immigrant visas available through a lottery to people who come from countries with low rates of immigration to the United States. Of such visas, 5,000 are allocated for use under NACARA beginning with DV '99.

The State Department (DOS) holds the lottery every year, and randomly selects approximately 110,000 applicants from all qualified entries. The DOS selects the approximately 110,000 applications since many will not complete the visa process.

However once 55,000 are issued or the fiscal year ends, the DV program is closed. If you receive a visa through the Diversity Visa Lottery Program you will be authorized to live and work permanently in the United States. You will also be allowed to bring your spouse and any unmarried children under the age of 21 to the United States.

NOTE

If you entered the United States illegally or you are affected by any of the inadmissibility rules, you may not be admitted into the United States even if you win the visa lottery. (See Chapter Seven for the inadmissibility rules.)

PHYSICIANS IN UNDERSERVED AREAS

Physicians who are in underserved areas may apply for change of status to a lawful permanent resident. Qualified physicians may apply personally (self sponsored) or through a United States employer. The national interest waiver for physicians in underserved areas relieves the petitioner only from the labor certification process. Petitioner may qualify if:

- A petitioner requesting a national interest waiver on behalf of a qualified alien physician, or

- An alien physician self-petitioning for second preference classification, based on medical service in a Health and Human Services Department (HHS)-designated underserved area or a Department of Veterans Affairs (VA) facility, you still must meet all eligibility requirements for this immigrant classification in order to be eligible for the national interest waiver.

<u>NATIONAL INTEREST WAIVER REQUIREMENTS</u>

The petitioner or self-petitioner must submit the following evidence with Form I-140 to support the request for a national interest waiver. For physicians planning to divide the practice of full-time clinical medicine between more than one underserved areas, the following evidence must be submitted for each area of intended practice:

1. If the physician will be an employee, she may need to submit a full-time employment contract issued and dated within 6 months prior to the date the petition is filed, for the required period of clinical medical practice, or an employment commitment letter from a Veterans Affairs facility.

2. If the physician will establish his or her own practice, the physician's sworn statement committing to the full-time practice of clinical medicine for the required period, and describing the steps the physician has taken or intends to actually take to establish the practice.

3. Evidence that the physician will provide full-time clinical medical service in a geographical area or areas designated by the Secretary of Health and Human Services as having a shortage of health care professionals and in a medical specialty that is within the scope of the Secretary's designation for the geographical area or areas, or in a facility under the jurisdiction of the Secretary of Veterans Affairs.

4. A letter issued and dated within 6 months prior to the date on which the petition is filed, from a Federal agency or the department of public health or equivalent of a State, including territories of the United States and the District of Columbia,

attesting that the alien physician's work is or will be in the public interest.

In addition, any attestation from a Federal agency must reflect

- The agency's knowledge of the alien's qualifications and the agency's background in making determinations on matters involving medical affairs so as to substantiate the finding that the alien's work is or will be in the public interest.

- An attestation from the public health department of a State, United States territory, or the District of Columbia must reflect that the agency has jurisdiction over the place where the alien physician intends to practice clinical medicine. If the alien physician intends to practice clinical medicine in more than one underserved area, attestations from each intended area of practice must be included. Attestations from the public health department of a State, United States territory, or the District of Columbia that does not have jurisdiction over the place in which the alien physician intends to practice clinical medicine will not be accepted.

<u>NOTE</u>

1. If the physician already has authorization to accept employment other than as a J-1 exchange alien, the beneficiary physician must complete an aggregate 5 years of qualifying full-time clinical practice during the 6-year period beginning on the date of approval of the Form I-140.

2. If the physician must obtain authorization to accept employment before the physician may lawfully begin working, the physician must complete the aggregate 5 years of qualifying full-time clinical practice during the 6-year period beginning on the date the Service issues the necessary employment authorization document.

CHAPTER SIX
RELIGIOUS WORKERS

There are two categories of Religious worker. They are the temporary or non-immigrant Religious Worker (R-1) and the permanent or Immigrant Religious worker.

DEFINITIONS OF RELIGIOUS WORKERS

Religious workers include ministers of religion who are authorized by a recognized denomination to conduct religious worship and perform other duties usually performed by members of the clergy such as administering the sacraments, or their equivalent. The term does not apply to lay preachers.

Religious vocation means a calling to religious life, evidenced by the demonstration of a lifelong commitment, such as taking of vows. Examples include nuns, monks, and religious brothers and sisters. Religious occupation means a habitual engagement in an activity, which relates to a traditional religious function. Examples include liturgical workers, religious instructors or cantors, catechists, workers in religious hospitals, missionaries, religious translators, or religious broadcasters.

It does not include janitors, maintenance workers, clerks, fundraisers, solicitors of donations, or similar occupations. The activity of a layperson that will be engaged in a religious occupation must relate to a traditional religious function.

The activity must embody the tenets of the religion and have religious significance, relating primarily, if not exclusively, to matters of the spirit as they apply to the religion.

MAJOR DIFFERENCE IN THE REQUIREMENTS OF NON IMMIGRANT (R-1) AND IMMIGRANT (GREEN CARD) CATEGORIES

Having defined a Religious worker, it is necessary to distinguish between the requirements of non-immigrant (R-1) and immigrant (Green Card) categories. There is a thin but very important line between the two categories.

NON-IMMIGRANT (R-1) CATEGORY

In this category, the beneficiary must have been for a minimum period of two years, **a member** of a religious denomination, which has a bona fide nonprofit, religious organization in the United States, and seeks to enter the U.S. to work solely:

- As a minister of that denomination or

- In a professional capacity in a religious vocation or occupation for that organization or

- In a religious vocation or occupation for the organization or its nonprofit affiliate.

IMMIGRANT CATEGORY (GREEN CARD)

Here, the beneficiary must have been **a member of the religious denominations for a minimum period of two years and has been carrying on the vocation, professional work, or other work described below, continuously for the past two years, on a full time basis,** and seek to enter the United States solely to work:

- As a minister of that denomination or

- In a professional capacity in a religious vocation or occupation for that organization or

- In a religious vocation or occupation for the organization or its nonprofit affiliate.

The basic difference is that for non- immigrant (R-1) category, the requirement is two-year membership. On the other hand, for immigrant (Green Card) category, the requirement is two-year full time employment as a religious worker immediately preceding the date of the application.

Immigration is very strict with this requirement when it comes to Immigrant or permanent status

In the case of non-immigrant or temporary status, the employer must file the petition using Form I-129. The petition must be accompanied by proof of Tax-Exempt status and a letter from the petitioner showing that the beneficiary is qualify as stated above.

In the case of Immigrant or permanent status, any person, including the applicant, can file a Form I-360 petition with the U.S. Bureau of Citizenship and Immigration Services in the Department of Homeland Security (BCIS) once she meets the religious worker criteria.

A petition for a person who is not a minister may only be filed until October 1, 2008, and any immigrant visa issued to such person shall not be valid beyond October 1, 2008. After the petition is approved by the CIS, the applicant can then file Form I-485. The I-360 petition must be accompanied by:

1. A letter from the authorized official of the religious organization establishing that the proposed services and applicant qualify as stated above

2. A letter from the authorized official of the religious organization attesting to the applicant's membership in the religious denomination and explaining,

in detail, the person's religious work and all employment during the past two years, and for the proposed employment

3. Evidence establishing that the religious organization, and any affiliate which will employ the person, is a bona fide nonprofit religious organization in the U.S. and is exempt from taxation under Section 501(c)(3) of the Internal Revenue Code of 1986.

4. Evidence that the alien has been on full time employment with the Religious Organization for the last two years immediately preceding the filing of the application.

Religious worker's spouse and unmarried children under 21 years of age may be granted derivative immigration status.

CHAPTER SEVEN
INELIGIBILITY

The immigration laws of the United States, in order to protect the health, welfare, and security of the United States, prohibit the issuance of a visa to certain applicants. Examples of applicants who must be refused visas are those who:

- Have a communicable disease such as tuberculosis, or

- Have a dangerous physical and mental disorder, or

- Are drug addicts

- Have committed serious criminal acts

- Are terrorists, subversives, members of a totalitarian party, or former Nazi war criminals

- Have used illegal means to enter the United States, or

- Are ineligible for citizenship. Some former exchange visitors must live abroad for 2 years. If found to be ineligible, the consular officer will then advise the applicant if the law provides for some form of waiver.

CHAPTER EIGHT
HOW TO BECOME
A U.S. CITIZEN

There are basically three methods to become a U. S. Citizen. An applicant may qualify under any of the three methods. The methods are:

BY BIRTH

Under the United States Constitution, any person born in the U.S. automatically becomes a U.S. Citizen. The legal status of the parents is immaterial concerning this issue. The fact that one or both parents are illegal immigrant will not affect the child's status as a Citizen of the United States for as long as the child was born in the U.S.

BY NATURALIZATION

The second method by which an alien may become a U.S. Citizen is by Naturalization. Naturalization is the next stage for a lawful permanent resident. However, it must be pointed out that naturalization is not automatic. There are certain conditions attached to being a permanent resident before an alien could become a citizen of the United States.

♦ Alien must have been a permanent resident for a minimum period of five years. However, if the alien is married to a United States citizen, the waiting period is reduced to three years. It must be pointed out that the marriage must be current. If the alien is divorced, she will have to wait for five years.

In addition, in the case of certain military veterans, the waiting period is also reduced to three years. Alien must be present in the United States for at least 50% of the residency period to qualify for citizenship. **NOTE:** If the alien served in the U.S. military during wartime, there is no residency required for citizenship.

♦ Alien must demonstrate loyalty to the United States.

♦ Alien must be of good moral character.

♦ Alien must not have a criminal record. If you have been involved in any form of crime as a lawful permanent resident, it is advisable that you consult with a competent immigration Attorney before applying for citizenship, otherwise, you may find yourself in your home country after filing the application.

♦ Alien must be able to communicate in basic elementary English (speak, read, write, and understand).

♦ Alien is required to take a short test on U.S. Government and History

DERIVATION

The third method of becoming a United States citizen is by derivation. Minor children of United States citizen born outside the U.S. may become U.S. citizen by derivation if both parents are United States citizen, and both have lived in the United States for some years before the children are born.

In addition, children born outside the United States may apply for citizenship in the United States if the parents naturalized while they are still minor.

PROOF OF CITIZENSHIP

For the purpose of immigration filings, there are two categories of proof of citizenship. They are the primary proof and the secondary proof.

PRIMARY PROOF

If you are born in the U.S., a copy of your birth certificate, issued by the civil registrar, vital statistics office, or other civil authority will suffice.

If you become a U.S. citizen by naturalization, proof of citizenship is the Certificate of Naturalization. In both cases, U.S. passport will suffice.

SECONDARY PROOF

Usually, secondary evidence is accepted only for people born in the United States. These includes:

- Church records. Documents bearing the seal of the church, showing the baptism, dedication or comparable rite which occurred within two months of birth, showing the date and place of the child's birth, date of the religious ceremony and the name of the child's parents

- School record. A letter from the authority of the first school attended, showing the date of admission to the school, child's date of birth at that time or age at that time, the place of birth, and the name of the parents.

- Census record. State or Federal census record showing the names, place of birth, date of birth or the age of the person listed.

- Affidavits. Written statements sworn to or affirmed by two persons who were living at the time and who have personal knowledge of the event you are trying to prove. The person making the affidavit does not have to be a citizen of the United States. The affidavit must contain a complete detail of how the person acquired knowledge of the event.

CHAPTER NINE
USEFUL WEBSITES

The following websites may be useful to you during your stay in the United States.

1. United States White House
   www.whitehouse.gov

2. United States Immigration
   www.uscis.gov

3. United States Department of state
   www.state.gov

4. United States Department of Homeland security   www.dhs.gov

5. United States Immigration and Custom Enforcement   www.ice.gov

6. United States Customs and Border protection   www.cbp.gov

7. United States Department of Justice www.usdoj.gov

8. United States department of Labor www.dol.gov

9. Social Security Administration www.ssa.gov

10. United States Embassies and Missions Abroad   www.usembassy.state.gov

11. United States Customs Service www.customs.gov

About the Author

The author is an Attorney from Nigeria. He practised Law in Nigeria for a decade before he came to the United States. He is licensed by the Supreme Court of New York. He is currently practising Immigration Law in Arlington, Texas. He is also a worker at The Redeemed Christian Church of God, Household of Faith, in Arlington, Texas.